j597.6
R35a

DETROIT PUBLIC LIBRARY

P9-CCV-403

DETROIT PUBLIC LIBRARY
CHASE BRANCH LIBRARY
17731 W. SEVEN MILE RD.
DETROIT, MI 48235

**DATE DUE**

JUN 06 1994

DEC 06 1994

OCT 3 1 2000

APR 2 0 1995

JUN 13 1995

APR 2 7 1998

JUN 0 1 1998

SEP 2 9 1998

MAY 2 9 1998

APR 1 0 2000

MAY 2 3 2000

APR - - 1994    CH

# OUR LIVING WORLD

# Amphibians

*By* **Edward R. Ricciuti**

*With Illustrations by* Pedro Julio González

*Series Editor:* Vincent Marteka
Introduction by John Behler, *New York Zoological Society*

**A BLACKBIRCH PRESS BOOK**
WOODBRIDGE, CONNECTICUT

Published by Blackbirch Press, Inc.
One Bradley Road, Suite 205
Woodbridge, CT 06525

©1993 Blackbirch Press, Inc.
First Edition

All rights reserved. No part of this book may be reproduced in any form without permission in writing from Blackbirch Press, Inc., except by a reviewer.

Printed in Canada

10 9 8 7 6 5 4 3 2 1

**Editorial Director:** Bruce Glassman
**Editor:** Geraldine C. Fox
**Editorial Assistant:** Michelle Spinelli
**Design Director:** Sonja Kalter
**Production:** Sandra Burr, Rudy Raccio

**Library of Congress Cataloging-in-Publication Data**

Ricciuti, Edward R.
    Amphibians / by Edward R. Ricciuti; introduction by John Behler.—1st ed.
        p.    cm. — (Our living world)
    Includes bibliographical references and index.
    Summary: Explores the senses, metabolism, and reproduction of amphibians.
    ISBN 1-56711-045-2
    1. Amphibians—Juvenile literature. [1. Amphibians.] I. Title. II. Series.
QL644.2.R515    1993
597.6—dc20                                                          93-20658
                                                                        CIP
                                                                         AC

# Contents

# What Does It Mean to Be "Alive"?

## Introduction by John Behler,
*New York Zoological Society*

One summer morning, as I was walking through a beautiful field, I was inspired to think about what it really means to be "alive." Part of the answer, I came to realize, was right in front of my eyes.

The meadow was ablaze with color, packed with wildflowers at the height of their blooming season. A multitude of insects, warmed by the sun's early-morning rays, began to stir. Painted turtles sunned themselves on an old mossy log in a nearby pond. A pair of wood ducks whistled a call as they flew overhead, resting near a shagbark hickory on the other side of the pond.

As I wandered through this unspoiled habitat, I paused at a patch of milkweed to look for monarch-butterfly caterpillars, which depend on the milkweed's leaves for food. Indeed, the caterpillars were there, munching away. Soon these larvae would spin their cocoons, emerge as beautiful orange-and-black butterflies, and begin a fantastic 1,500-mile (2,400-kilometer) migration to wintering grounds in Mexico. It took biologists nearly one hundred years to unravel the life history of these butterflies. Watching them in the milkweed patch made me wonder how much more there is to know about these insects and all the other living organisms in just that one meadow.

The patterns of the natural world have often been likened to a spider's web, and for good reason. All life on Earth is interconnected in an elegant yet surprisingly simple design, and each living thing is an essential part of that design. To understand biology and the functions of living things, biologists have spent a lot of time looking at the differences among organisms. But in order to understand the very nature of living things, we must first understand what they have in common.

The butterfly larvae and the milkweed—and all animals and plants, for that matter—are made up of the same basic elements. These elements are obtained, used, and eliminated by every living thing in a series of chemical activities called metabolism.

Every molecule of every living tissue must contain carbon. During photosynthesis, green plants take in carbon dioxide from the atmosphere. Within their chlorophyll-filled leaves, in the presence of sunlight, the carbon dioxide is combined with water to form sugar—nature's most basic food. Animals need carbon, too. To grow and function, animals must eat plants or other animals that have fed on plants in order to obtain carbon. When plants and animals die, bacteria and fungi help to break down their tissues. This allows the carbon in plants and animals to be recycled. Indeed, the carbon in your body—and everyone else's body—may once have been inside a dinosaur, a giant redwood, or a monarch butterfly!

All life also needs nitrogen. Nitrogen is an essential component of protoplasm, the complex of chemicals that makes up living cells. Animals acquire nitrogen in the same manner as they acquire carbon dioxide: by eating plants or other animals that have eaten plants. Plants, however, must rely on nitrogen-fixing bacteria in the soil to absorb nitrogen from the atmosphere and convert it into proteins. These proteins are then absorbed from the soil by plant roots.

Living things start life as a single cell. The process by which cells grow and reproduce to become a specific organism—whether the organism is an oak tree or a whale—is controlled by two basic substances called deoxyribonucleic acid (DNA) and ribonucleic acid (RNA). These two chemicals are the building blocks of genes that determine how an organism looks, grows, and functions. Each organism has a unique pattern of DNA and RNA in its genes. This pattern determines all the characteristics of a living thing. Each species passes its unique pattern from generation to generation. Over many billions of years, a process involving genetic mutation and natural selection has allowed species to adapt to a constantly changing environment by evolving—changing genetic patterns. The living creatures we know today are the results of these adaptations.

Reproduction and growth are important to every species, since these are the processes by which new members of a species are created. If a species cannot reproduce and adapt, or if it cannot reproduce fast enough to replace those members that die, it will become extinct (no longer exist).

In recent years, biologists have learned a great deal about how living things function. But there is still much to learn about nature. With high-technology equipment and new information, exciting discoveries are being made every day. New insights and theories quickly make many biology textbooks obsolete. One thing, however, will forever remain certain: As living things, we share an amazing number of characteristics with other forms of life. As animals, our survival depends upon the food and functions provided by other animals and plants. As humans—who can understand the similarities and interdependence among living things—we cannot help but feel connected to the natural world, and we cannot forget our responsibility to protect it. It is only through looking at, and understanding, the rest of the natural world that we can truly appreciate what it means to be "alive."

# Amphibians: The Overview

It is a spring evening in southern New England. Raindrops from a passing shower spatter the surface of a woodland pond, which will be dry by late summer. At the edge of the pond, a frog, small enough to sit on a nickel, lies in the water, its head above the surface. Suddenly, the white skin of the frog's throat swells into a glistening bubble. From the tiny frog comes a series of clear, peeping sounds that ring through the darkness.

The frog, a spring peeper, belongs to a class of vertebrates (animals that have backbones) known as amphibians. The term *amphibian* is from two Greek words, *amphi*, meaning "both," and *bios*, meaning "life." This refers to the fact that most amphibians lead a double life—existing first as water-breathers and then as air-breathers on land. Most hatch from eggs in the water and spend the first part of their lives there, removing oxygen from the water with their

*Opposite:*
A red-eyed tree frog climbs up the stem of a green plant. Most amphibians have the ability to live both in water and on land.

gills. As they grow into adults, they develop the ability to move on land and breathe air. Some adults then spend part of their lives, or all of their lives, on land.

## The Amazing Variety of Amphibians

The spring peeper is among the more than 4,000 known species (kinds) of amphibians. The 3,800 species of frogs and toads form the largest of the three amphibian groups, or orders. Salamanders make up the second group, and the worm-like caecilians make up the third, and smallest, group. Frogs and toads have long hind legs, with five toes on each foot, and small forelegs, with four toes each. The toes of tree frogs—including the spring peeper—are tipped with suction disks that help them climb. A peeper can even walk up a smooth windowpane. The feet of most frogs are webbed, which helps them swim. On land, their muscular hind legs give them great leaping power. The cricket frog, which is 1 1/2 inches (4 centimeters) long, can travel 40 times its own length in one jump!

*Below, right*: Salamanders, like this young red-spotted newt, are one of the three major orders of amphibians. *Below, left*: Frogs, like this green mosaic frog, and toads make up the largest of the three groups of amphibians.

Salamanders, of which there are approximately 340 species, are lizard-like animals with long, slim bodies, long tails, and four legs. The legs of most salamanders are short and stick out to the side. They are not built for fast movement. Salamanders walk over the ground slowly—in water they creep along the bottom and among plants. They swim by means of their tail, which acts as an oar. Typical salamanders have the same number of toes as frogs and toads.

Some large salamanders that spend all their lives in water have bodies that vary from the standard salamander shape. The mud puppy has a chunky body with four toes on each foot; the hellbender also has a thick body, with a broad, flat head; the amphiuma is snake-like, with tiny legs; and the siren, which resembles an eel, lacks hind limbs.

Although they look like eels or snakes, sirens are a kind of salamander that spend their lives entirely in the water.

Amphibians: The Overview

There are only about 75 species of caecilians. They live mostly underground, they lack limbs, and the series of ring-like segments on their bodies makes them resemble earthworms. They look nothing like frogs or salamanders.

Most amphibians are rather small. The smallest amphibian is probably the Cuban pygmy frog, which

Caecilians, which live mostly underground, make up the smallest group of amphibians. They are characterized by long, thin, segmented bodies and do not have any legs.

Above, left: The largest frog is the Goliath frog of Africa. A large Goliath frog can grow up to 3 feet (1 meter) long and weigh up to 7 pounds (3 kilograms). *Above, right:* The giant webbed foot of a Goliath frog makes it a swift and powerful swimmer.

is less than 1/2 inch (1 centimeter) long. A 12-inch (30-centimeter) amphibian is considered big, but a few amphibians are much larger. The largest living species is a giant salamander that grows to more than 5 feet (2 meters) long, and lives in streams in Japan and China. The monster among frogs is the Goliath frog of Africa, which measures 3 feet (1 meter) in length and weighs 7 pounds (3 kilograms). One caecilian reaches 4 1/2 feet (more than 1 meter), although it is no bigger around than a man's thumb.

## The First Amphibians

Amphibians evolved, or developed, from primitive fishes—the first vertebrate animals—more then 300 million years ago. Then reptiles developed from amphibians, and birds and mammals developed from reptiles.

Amphibians were the first creatures capable of living on land and breathing air. As they moved from water to land, they found themselves in a fresh environment that was more favorable to their development than the water, where many life-forms competed with one another. Amphibians had few enemies on land. They shared it with insects and spiders, which served as their food.

Amphibians: The Overview

As amphibians became partly adapted to life on land, they evolved into a great variety of forms, many of which have become extinct (died out). Most had long bodies like the modern salamander and were about the same size. A few grew to a very large size—8 feet (2 meters). Like today's amphibians, some remained in water all the time, while others, with better legs and an increased ability to maintain moist skin, spent much of their time on land.

Amphibians are no longer the dominant land creatures that they once were. Together, their descendants—reptiles, birds, and mammals—have taken over the land, while fishes continue to dominate the Earth's waters.

## *Amphibian Habitats*

Amphibians can be found almost everywhere on Earth, although some are very limited as to where they make their homes. Because they are adapted for life both on land and in water, they often live where two habitats, land and water, for example, meet—places called ecotones. Most salamanders live in the Northern Hemisphere, while caecilians inhabit a belt across tropical South America, Africa, and Asia. Frogs and toads are the most widespread amphibians. They live on every continent except Antarctica, as well as on many islands. Frogs and toads are most abundant in the tropics. Two square miles (5 square kilometers) of South American rain forest can have more than 80 different species of frogs. Twenty species is a very large number for the same amount of territory in North America.

It is not uncommon for species of amphibians to inhabit a rather limited range. The Valdina Farms salamander, for example, lives exclusively in a single water-filled sinkhole on a Texas farm. The red-cheeked

**In Living Color**

Many amphibians are just as colorful as birds or fishes. The spotted salamander is jet black and has bright yellow spots. Some tropical frogs are vivid red and black. The little Pine Barrens tree frog has a body that is mostly lime green, with a purple stripe that is edged with white running along its body and legs. The undersides of its legs are orange.

## *Fun Froggy Facts*

The flying frog of Borneo can launch itself high above the ground and soar through the air, using its huge webbed feet as parachutes.

The South American horned frog is one of a group of species that burrow into the ground when the rainy season ends. Once they are in the ground, they encase themselves in cocoons that cover their entire body, except for the two small air vents. The cocoon looks like parchment and is made of layers of dried skin and mucus. Once in a cocoon, a frog can live for many months waiting for the rains to begin again.

The spadefoot toad has a hard edge on the inside of its two hind feet that it uses to burrow backward into the ground.

The gopher frog of the southeastern United States actually lives in the burrows of another kind of animal—the gopher tortoise.

The red-eyed tree frog has first and second fingers and toes (much like human thumbs and forefingers). This finger structure enables the red-eyed tree frog to grasp twigs and branches quickly and easily as it flies through the air like a monkey.

The wood frog lives further north than any other frog or toad in North America.  It is even found in pools way up in Alaska.

South African painted reed frogs and their relatives have skin that is extremely sensitive to light, temperature, humidity, and their own mood. Like their reptile cousin, the chameleon, the reed frog's appearance can change in an instant to adapt to changes in the surroundings. If a reed frog wants to attract a mate, it will show off its bright and attractive colors. If it is exposed to bright lights, however, the frog will turn pale.

**Spadefoot toad**

**Wood frog**

salamander lives only within the Great Smoky Mountains National Park. The Roanoke salamander makes its home in a handful of caves in the mountains of southwestern Virginia.  And the Georgia blind salamander inhabits only a few underground pools,

The Georgia blind salamander's habitat is in dark places, such as underground pools and streams. Because of its lightless surroundings, this species of salamander has lost its eyesight as it has evolved over thousands of years.

DID YOU KNOW

**Mind-Froggling**

Have you ever wondered what the difference is between a frog and a toad? The answer is very little, really! The very same animal may be called a frog in one part of the world and a toad in another. Scientists who classify and study amphibians don't use either term anymore. Instead, they use the Latin scientific names.

streams, and wells in a small part of southeastern Georgia and nearby Florida. Like some other animals that live in the darkness of caves, this salamander has lost the use of its eyes.

Other amphibians have a very extensive range. The bullfrog is native to almost the entire southern, eastern, and central United States and has been introduced by people throughout the West. The range of the tiger salamander covers most of the United States and spills over into Mexico and Canada. In parts of the Midwest and dry Southwest, it is the only native salamander.

Wherever they make their homes, amphibians are most common in wet places and least common in dry areas, especially in cold climates.

## Amphibian Features

Millions of years ago, when amphibians evolved from fishes, they shared several characteristics of their ancestors. As time passed, however, they began to look less and less like fishes and adapted their own special features. All amphibians, whether frogs or toads, salamanders or newts, or caecilians, have these characteristics.

**Backbones** The amphibian skeleton shares a number of traits with other vertebrates. Like people, horses, lizards, goldfishes, and eagles, a frog has a bony skeleton. The skeleton is the body's framework, supporting the body, sheltering organs, and anchoring the muscles. An adult amphibian's skeleton is built on the same pattern as that of humans and other vertebrates. It centers around the backbone, a column down the middle of the back. The spinal cord, which contains nerves connected to the brain and other parts of the body, runs through the middle of the backbone. The backbone of long-bodied vertebrates can contain an astonishing number of vertebrae (bones). Certain species of salamanders have about 100 vertebrae, and some caecilians have more than 200. Frogs and toads, which lack a neck and are not long like caecilians and most salamanders, have only 6 to 10 vertebrae. (The human backbone has 26.)

**Cold-bloodedness** Amphibians, like fishes and reptiles, are cold-blooded animals. This means that they cannot produce very much body heat—as can warm-blooded birds and mammals—but must derive warmth from their surroundings. That means, in a warm place, an amphibian's body temperature will go up, and in a cool place it will go down. Because of this, an amphibian must spend energy seeking places that will keep its body temperature stable.

**Moist, slimy skin** Amphibians have moist, slimy skin, unlike their reptile descendants, which have dry, scaly skin. This moist skin serves mostly as an aid to breathing. There are even some amphibians that,

**DID YOU KNOW**

**Izard a Lizard?**

People frequently mistake salamanders for lizards, which are reptiles. At a glance, their bodies look very similar. Up close, however, you can easily see two major differences. Like all amphibians, a salamander has smooth skin, while reptiles are scaly. And, unlike reptiles, amphibians do not have claws on their feet.

# Internal Anatomy of a Frog

HEART

LUNG

LIVER

OVARY

STOMACH

SMALL INTESTINE

ABDOMINAL VEIN

BLADDER

LARGE INTESTINE

SPINE (backbone)

VERTEBRAE

SKULL

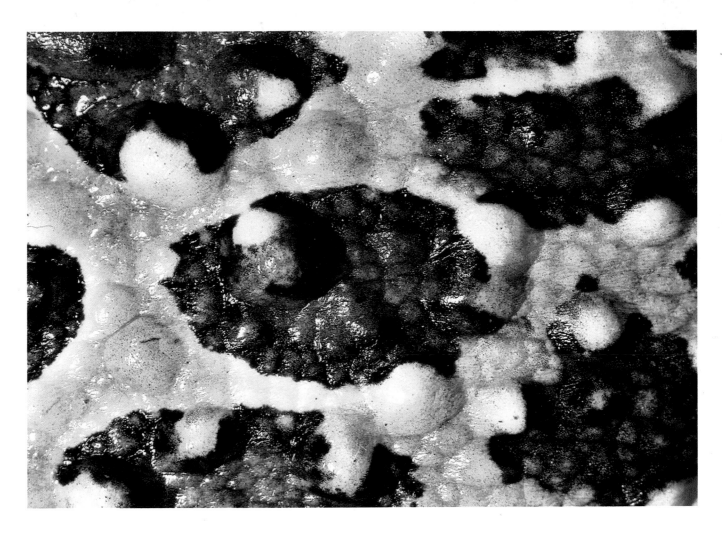

because they lack lungs, rely on their skin as the major organ of respiration (the exchange of gases with the atmosphere). The sliminess is caused by secretions of mucous glands. The skin of most amphibians also contains poison glands, which help amphibians to defend themselves against predators.

**Teeth** Most amphibians have teeth on the rims of their jaws or the roof of their mouth. A frog, for example, has a few teeth on the roof of its mouth and others along the edge of its outer jaw. Amphibian teeth are tiny; some are so small that they cannot be seen without the aid of a microscope. Amphibians do not use their teeth to chew or bite, since they swallow their prey whole. The role of the teeth is probably to grip slippery prey, such as worms. There are a few exceptions, however. The big horned frog of South America uses its teeth to deliver a nasty bite.

A close-up of horned frog skin. Amphibians have mucous glands that keep their skin moist and slimy. Many amphibians also have poison glands in their skin, which secrete poisons that help to protect the animals from enemies.

# 2

# *The Senses: How Amphibians React*

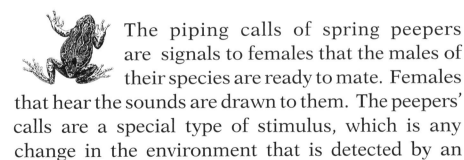 The piping calls of spring peepers are signals to females that the males of their species are ready to mate. Females that hear the sounds are drawn to them. The peepers' calls are a special type of stimulus, which is any change in the environment that is detected by an animal's sense organs.

Amphibians have the same five basic senses that you have—sight, hearing, smell, taste, and touch. These senses are flooded by stimuli from the amphibian's surroundings. An animal will generally react to a particular stimulus in a certain way. The reaction, or response, of the female spring peeper is to head for the source of mating calls. A movement that could signal the presence of an enemy is another type of stimulus to the peeper. If she is to survive, her response must be one that helps her avoid danger, such as hiding or jumping away.

*Opposite:*
A leopard frog leaps high out of the water. Amphibians, like all living things, use their senses to respond to stimuli in their environment.

Stimuli are like messages. The movement of a fly on a leaf is a message to a frog's eyes. If the eyes receive it, the message passes through one set of nerves to the brain. The brain then processes the information and sends out an order through other nerves to muscles in the frog's mouth and jaws. If the order gets through as it should, the frog reacts by trying to snap up the fly. The brain and the nerves that control and process stimuli and responses make up an animal's nervous system.

The time between the reception of a stimulus and a response can be almost instantaneous. (If you accidentally touch a hot stove, you draw your finger back in a flash. You don't think about it. You just do it.) Some stimuli, however, are gradual. The increase in the hours of daylight during the spring, for example, slowly causes chemical changes in a spring peeper's body that prepare it for mating.

Some amphibians rely more on certain sense organs than others. Frogs have very good ears, while salamanders can barely hear at all. However, both see well and rely heavily on vision, especially to find food.

Though some amphibians rely heavily on their ability to hear, salamanders can hardly hear at all. Instead, they rely primarily on their eyesight for survival.

The eyes of most amphibians work in much the same way that human eyes do. Both kinds of eyes have lenses, retinas, and light-sensitive cells called rods and cones.

## *How Amphibians See*

Like the eyes of other vertebrates, amphibian eyes work much like a camera. Light enters the eye through a clear structure called a lens. To focus at different distances, the lens changes shape. An amphibian's lens, like that of a fish, is not flexible. It pulls back to focus on a far-off object and moves forward to see something up close.

At the rear of the eye is a light-sensitive coating called the retina. It acts like film behind the lens of a camera and registers light that enters the eye. The information received by the retina races through the nervous system to the brain, where the information is "developed" into a "picture."

The amphibian retina, like yours, contains two types of vision cells, named according to their shapes. Cells called rods are sensitive to light. In darkness, many rods come to the surface of the retina. In bright light, cones, which are not as light-sensitive, replace

**DID YOU KNOW**

**Eye-Catchers**

Salamanders have a hard time catching some of the quick creatures that frogs and toads can grab. A slow-moving salamander must be very near its prey to catch it. Perhaps not surprisingly, salamanders are believed to have better close-up vision than frogs and toads. Frogs and toads react swiftly to movement, but not to something that is still. A fly can freeze just inches away from a toad and escape attack. Once the fly twitches, the toad makes its move.

## Cheers for Tears

In a sense, amphibians were the first animals to cry. The eyes of fish, from which amphibians arose, are kept moist by the water around them. A fish's eye will dry out in the air. The early amphibians escaped this problem because they developed glands to keep their eyes moist. All land vertebrates have these eye glands. In people, these glands cause tears. Amphibians were also the first creatures on Earth to have eyelids, which help prevent drying of the eyes and protect against dust and dirt.

most of the rods. Cones also register color, and amphibians are believed to have color vision.

Most amphibians have a clear membrane that can be drawn across the eye to protect it. This allows most amphibians to see clearly underwater. Called the nictitating membrane, this structure is also present in birds and aquatic reptiles, such as the alligator.

Frogs, toads, and salamanders—except those that live in dark places—have good vision. Caecilians are nearly blind. Their eyes are covered by skin and sometimes by bone. Caecilians sense the presence of objects by means of chemical cues.

## How Amphibians Hear

Frogs and toads have excellent hearing. Their hearing is so sharp that they can pick up the sound of a footstep at a pond's edge. Sound travels as energy waves, a form of vibration, through matter, such as air and water. The vibrations are picked up by the eardrum, which is visible on each side of the head of frogs and toads. (They do not have outer ears, as you do.) The eardrum acts like a drum head, magnifying the vibrations, which are transmitted through a rod-shaped bone to the inner ear. There, the vibrations travel through fluid within a small chamber. Sensory

The Senses: How Amphibians React

nerves in the chamber then record vibrations and send the sound signals to the brain.

Salamanders and caecilians lack an eardrum and do not seem to be able to pick up sounds in the air. However, they do sense vibrations carried through water. Salamanders also pick up vibrations from the ground through their legs.

## The Senses of Smell, Taste, and Touch

In vertebrate animals such as amphibians, smell and taste are closely related. Cells to detect smell are located in the snout and nose of most amphibians. Tiny hairs on cells inside the nose vibrate, bringing in air or water, which carries odor-bearing molecules. Nerves then relay the information to the brain, where it is registered as a smell. Amphibians that live in water and in the soil have a much better sense of smell than those that live mostly on land. Before changing into adult form, young amphibians seem to have an exceptional sense of smell, perhaps as keen as that of fishes.

An amphibian can also smell by means of two chambers that open into the roof of its mouth. The amphibian's tongue brings scented chemical particles from its

Frogs and toads have visible eardrums to the rear of their eyes that look like round drum heads. These eardrums are extremely sensitive to vibration, giving frogs and toads very good hearing.

## The Voice Choice

The first voice that ever sounded on Earth belonged to an amphibian—not the first sound, but the first voice. Many animals make sounds. Some fishes grunt by releasing air from an air sac, and male field crickets chirp by running their wings together, but these sounds are not voices.

A voice can be produced only by a structure in the throat called a larynx, or voice box. In humans, speech is formed in the voice box, where two cords of elastic tissue, the vocal cords, vibrate like guitar strings when air passes over them. The voice box first appeared in amphibians. Among modern amphibians, only frogs and toads use the voice box to call, although some salamanders can squeak. Instead of cords, the larynx of a frog or toad has a pair of elastic lips.

A frog calls by closing its nostrils and mouth and sealing in air. It pumps the air between its lungs and voice box. As a frog calls, the skin of its throat expands into a "vocal sac" (some species have two sacs). The sound resounds in the sac and grows even louder. A group of spring peepers can be heard calling for up to 1/2 mile (1 kilometer) away!

**Spring peeper**

surroundings into the chambers, where cells that are sensitive to odor register the scents.

The amphibian's taste buds are located on its tongue and around its mouth. Scientists are unsure how sensitive the taste buds are, but adult frogs will sometimes spit out substances that seem to taste bad. Some of the bump-like taste buds on the tongue of a frog also may be related to the sense of touch.

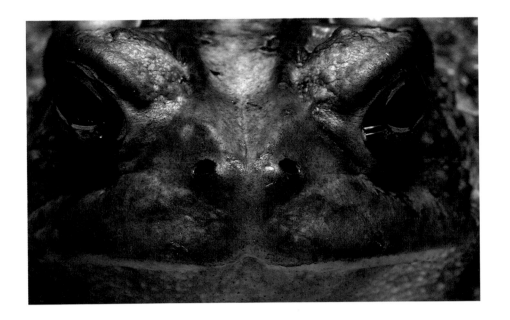

Most amphibians have odor-detecting cells in their snouts and noses. Once an odor acts as a stimulus to the nerves, the information is relayed to the brain, where it is registered as a smell.

Scattered over the skin of amphibians are nerve endings that sense touch. In addition, papillae, tiny projections whose cells can detect touch, are present on the feet and heads of frogs and on the lips of some salamanders.

Amphibian skin is also sensitive to chemical stimuli that are slightly irritating. This sensitivity may help amphibians determine how salty or acidic the water is. The skin of other vertebrates becomes irritated only where it is moistened by mucus, such as inside the nose. Your nose, for example, can become irritated by certain kinds of smoke.

## Drawing the Line on Amphibians

Like their fish ancestors, the mud puppy and several other aquatic amphibians have an organ called the lateral line, which serves as an extended sense of touch. The lateral line is a series of fluid-filled chambers in the skin along each side of the mud puppy. These chambers contain tiny hairs and nerve cells that open to the water through the skin's pores. Subsonic (very low) vibrations pass from the water through the pores into the fluid. The fluid moves, and the hairs pick up the vibrations. Nerve cells that are attached to the hairs then relay the information to the animal's brain.

The Senses: How Amphibians React

# 3

# Metabolism: How Amphibians Function

In the darkness of a spring night, a tiger prowls. Searching for food, it moves quietly through the forest. But the forest is not in Asia. It is in North America. And the tiger is only a foot long. It is a tiger salamander, as fierce a hunter in its world of the forest floor as a real tiger is in its own habitat.

As the salamander wanders through the dead leaves that carpet the forest floor, it encounters a nest holding a batch of newborn mice. The helpless mice will become food for the salamander.

All living things need food to fuel the body's many functions. Like other animals, amphibians use food to produce the energy they need to stay alive. Energy enables them to breathe, to walk and swim, to sleep, to grow and have young—and to seek more food.

Activities such as finding food and using it to make energy are part of a complex chemical process

*Opposite:*
A European toad lunges for an earthworm. All living things need food to produce the energy they need to survive.

## Let Sleeping Frogs Lie

People once believed that frogs fell from the sky during rainstorms. While this, of course, is not the case, the belief does have a basis in fact.

During droughts, or dry spells, amphibians often burrow deep in the ground, seeking cool temperatures and moisture. Once buried, their rate of metabolism drops very low. They seem in a deep sleep, even dead. Their heart beats slowly, and they have no need for food other than what is stored in their bodies. This condition is known as dormancy. In desert areas, which are dry, some amphibians spend most of the year underground in a dormant state. When rain falls, they awaken and head for the surface in great numbers. People who saw this happen to frogs were tricked into thinking that the frogs had fallen from the sky.

Amphibians also become dormant when they are in very cold areas. Since they can survive sub-freezing cold for only a matter of hours, those that live where the winters are cold become inactive and spend the season on the bottoms of ponds, under rocks and logs, and in the forest floor, where temperatures remain warmer than out in the open.

that goes on every minute that an animal is alive. This process is called metabolism.

Metabolism must work properly for an animal to survive. If something goes wrong with its metabolism, an animal will become sick and may even die. Some animals metabolize faster than others. The pace at which animals metabolize is called the rate of metabolism. Birds and mammals have a high rate of metabolism because they need lots of energy to produce body heat. Amphibians have a much lower rate of metabolism. They need less food, and they need it less frequently than do birds and mammals. Some amphibians can go for months without a meal.

On the other hand, an amphibian uses up energy moving around to keep its body at a safe temperature. When the temperature around an amphibian rises, so does its rate of metabolism. Then, it is more active and requires more food.

## What Amphibians Eat

Most amphibians are predators—that is, they eat other animals. Not all amphibians, however, start off as predators. Young frogs and toads (tadpoles) feed mainly on algae and water plants, although they do eat a few small animals. They also eat the remains of dead plants and animals. Their horny lips help them scrape algae off surfaces of rocks and leaves. Salamander tadpoles are fierce hunters, feeding on small water animals and, sometimes, one another.

Adult amphibians feed completely on animals—mainly invertebrates, such as insects, worms, and spiders—but they also eat fish, snakes, birds, rats, bats, and other amphibians. Bullfrogs sometimes swallow newborn ducklings. Snakes that try to eat bullfrogs may wind up being eaten—one bullfrog was found with a baby alligator in its stomach!

Frogs and toads often sit still, waiting to ambush prey. In Africa, the arum frog hides in the center of an arum lily, which, like the frog, is ivory-colored. The frog snaps up insects attracted to the lilies. When the lilies are not blooming, the frog's color turns dark, and it hides in other plants, waiting for a meal there.

DID YOU KNOW

**Pop-Eyes**

The eyes of a frog or toad help it to swallow food, especially large prey. The eyes are set in structures that give frogs and toads a pop-eyed appearance. When one of these animals swallows, its eyes close and are pulled back into its head. This process probably causes pressure that helps push the food down the animal's throat.

Most amphibians are meat-eaters. Here, a biting frog holds a rat it has captured after a scuffle.

A barred tiger salamander swallows an earthworm. Many adult amphibians feed primarily on invertebrates, such as insects, worms, and spiders.

## Digesting Food

An animal cannot use food until it is broken down into basic chemicals. The process of breaking down food is called digestion. Mammals begin to break down food as they eat it, by chewing it into small pieces. Amphibians, however, cannot chew their food, so they swallow it whole.

After an amphibian swallows food, the food passes down a flexible tube called the esophagus and into the stomach. Glands in the stomach then produce acids and other juices that start to chemically break down the food. Next, the food passes to the looped small intestine, where it is further digested before it is carried by water through the intestinal walls into the blood. Any undigested food is stored in the large intestine as waste until it is excreted (eliminated).

Metabolism: How Amphibians Function

## A Sticky Situation

Insects are the main prey of frogs and toads.  To capture insect prey, a frog or toad uses its sticky tongue, which is attached to the front of the mouth—not the rear, like yours—and folded backward.  The amphibian opens its mouth and flips its tongue out and up.  The tip of the tongue curls around the insect, and the insect sticks to the tongue as if the tongue were fly paper.  Then the tongue carries the insect back to the amphibian's mouth—and it all happens in a flash.

## The Digestive System of a Frog

ESOPHAGUS

STOMACH

KIDNEY

LARGE INTESTINE

LIVER

GALL BLADDER

PANCREAS

SMALL INTESTINE

BLADDER

ANUS

## How Amphibians Breathe

Like all other animals, amphibians need energy to function properly. Cells get this energy from food. To release energy from food, oxygen is needed. Most living organisms get oxygen by breathing.

Breathing, which is part of a constant process called respiration, is basically an exchange of gases between a living organism and the air or water around it. When an animal breathes in, oxygen enters its body. When it breathes out, carbon dioxide, the waste gas produced, leaves its body.

While all animals need oxygen, some get it in different ways than others. Most vertebrates breathe oxygen from the air and exchange it for carbon dioxide in their lungs. Oxygen enters the blood through the thin walls of blood vessels in the lungs. Carbon dioxide leaves in a reverse direction. Fishes obtain oxygen by passing water over delicate feathers of tissue called gills, located behind their heads. The exchange of gases takes place through blood vessels in these structures.

Like their close relatives, fishes, newly hatched amphibians, or tadpoles, also breathe through gills. The gills of frog and toad tadpoles are located within their heads. Those of salamander tadpoles are external and resemble little trees to the rear of their heads.

### Lung Time, No See

A frog takes air into its lungs by using muscles in its mouth. First it shuts its mouth and closes off the passage to the lungs. Next, it lowers the floor of its mouth, which draws air in through its nostrils. The frog then seals the nostrils, opens the way to the lungs, and returns the floor of its mouth to its original position. This causes the air to be pushed to the lungs. A frog may force one gulp of air back and forth several times before exhaling (breathing out).

During respiration, water enters a tadpole's mouth and then flows over the animal's gills. Once oxygen is exchanged for carbon dioxide, the water is expelled through a small hole that is on the left side of the tadpole's head.

Most adult amphibians use their lungs to breathe. The lungs of an amphibian, however, have less surface for blood vessels than those of other air-breathing vertebrates and are therefore less efficient. Several kinds of salamanders do not have lungs, so they must breathe in other ways. One way is through the skin. As long as an amphibian's skin is moist, oxygen and carbon dioxide can pass through it. Another place where these gases are exchanged is through blood vessels in an amphibian's mouth and throat.

A salamander larva swims quickly through the water. Like their relatives, fishes, newly hatched amphibians breathe through their gills, which look like tiny trees to the rear of their heads.

## Skintight

Dead or worn skin cuts down on the exchange of gases that amphibians need to breathe. Amphibians solve this problem by shedding their skin when it gets old. When a toad sheds its skin, it hunches its back and puffs up its body. The skin splits along the back and underside of the toad's body. Then, like a person taking off a sweater that feels too tight, the toad pushes and pulls the skin over its head with its legs. Once that job is done, the toad eats the old skin.

## Removing Wastes

All living things produce wastes during metabolism. The process by which these wastes are removed is called excretion.

Food wastes, the end products of digestion, are stored in the large intestine. They leave the body of an amphibian through the anus, which opens into a compartment called the cloaca. Urine, a waste that is produced by the animal's kidneys, also empties into the cloaca.

Carbon dioxide is a waste product of respiration. It passes out of an amphibian's body through the lungs and the moist outer skin that covers the body.

## Blood Circulation

The oxygen taken in during respiration is carried to the cells of an amphibian's body in blood. The blood travels through the body through blood vessels—veins and arteries. The muscular pump that moves the blood is the heart. Together, the blood vessels and the heart make up the circulatory system.

The heart of an amphibian has three chambers—the human heart has four. The two chambers on top are the right and left atria (singular, *atrium*). Below them lies the third chamber, or ventricle.

Blood carrying oxygen from the lungs flows to the left atrium through a series of veins. Deoxygenated,

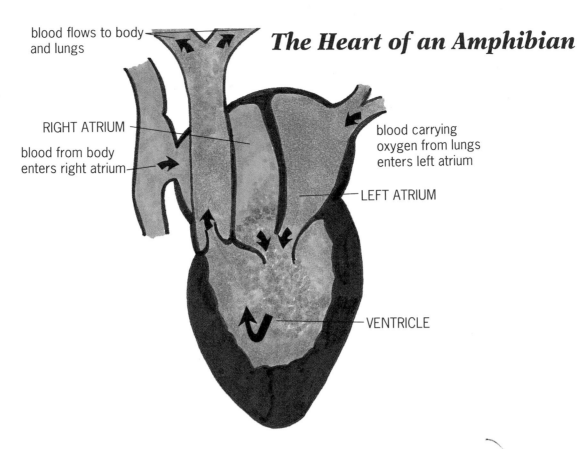

blood flows to body and lungs

## The Heart of an Amphibian

RIGHT ATRIUM

blood from body enters right atrium

blood carrying oxygen from lungs enters left atrium

LEFT ATRIUM

VENTRICLE

or spent, blood returns from the body to the right atrium through another system of veins. As the heart pumps, the right atrium empties oxygen-poor blood into the ventricle. An instant later, the left atrium forces its load of oxygenated blood into the ventricle. From there, a large artery sends spent blood to the lungs. Another artery then sends the fresh blood to the body.

Why don't the two kinds of blood mix in the ventricle? They do, but only a little. Entering first, the spent blood pools on the ventricle's right side. That is where the opening leading out of the ventricle is located. When the heart pumps again, the spent blood leaves the ventricle ahead of the fresh blood.

Strands of muscle between the right and left sides of the ventricle also help prevent blood from mixing. Your ventricle, and that of birds and some reptiles, is completely divided into two chambers—a right one and a left one—so the two types of blood never come in contact with each other.

Metabolism: How Amphibians Function

# 4

# *Reproduction and Growth*

*Quackety, quackety, quackety.*
*Preep, preep, preep.*
*Waaaah.*

Gibberish? Not to frogs and toads. These are some of the sounds made by male frogs and toads to attract females for mating.

Mating is part of reproduction, the process by which a species makes members of its own kind. A species can survive only by reproducing from one generation to the next. If it does not, it will die out.

## *Preparing to Mate*

Like many other animals, some amphibians mate only at certain times of year, often for a short period or even just once. In temperate regions—areas where it is neither very hot nor very cold—most amphibians mate during the spring and early summer. In the warmer climates of the tropics, amphibians of one

*Opposite:*
A pair of tree frogs mate in the protective covering of a patch of amplexus, a ground cover. Reproduction is one of the most important functions of any living thing because it is the key to keeping a species in existence.

**37**

## A Frog in the Throat

People often mistake the mating calls of male frogs and toads for those of other animals, such as insects or birds. The quackety, quackety, quackety of wood frogs makes them sound like ducks, and the preep, preep, preep of the spring peeper is sometimes mistaken for the twittering of songbirds or crickets. From a distance, the noises made by a group of peepers sound like sleigh bells. Waaaah, the call of the Fowler's toad, reminds some people of an insect.

kind or another mate year-round. Most mate in water, but a few amphibians mate on land.

In preparation for mating, changes take place in an amphibian's body. These changes are caused by chemicals called hormones. The body produces sex cells, and changes in its outward appearance may occur—its colors may brighten, for example.

The chemical changes that lead to mating are caused by various stimuli in the environment. These stimuli include increasing hours of sunlight, warmer temperatures, and concentrated rainfall.

## Meeting a Mate

Amphibians have little to do with one another outside of mating time. Many keep to themselves, but for reproduction to occur, something has to bring the male and female amphibians together—in ponds, in streams, and in other bodies of water. First, most amphibians seek out water in which to mate. Then they must find mates of their own species.

The red-spotted newt lives in the same pond all year. Thus, male and female are already in a place where they can mate. But what about the spring peeper, which has spent the winter burrowing in the forest floor? In ways not completely understood, but involving several senses, males and females gather in the water. Many amphibians return to the same body of water every year. Some return to the very place in which they hatched. Scientists suspect that the smell

Sound is an important stimulus to most amphibians during the mating season. Male spring peepers, for example, have an elaborate mating call that is understood and answered only by the female of the species.

of dampness and even landmarks may help them zero in on their mating grounds. Instinct—behavior inherited from ancestors—also plays a role.

Sound is an important stimulus for frogs and toads at mating time. The male of each species has its own special mating call. Males arrive in the water first and start calling. They sing together in a loud chorus that fills the night with sound.

Hundreds, even thousands, of frogs and toads of several species, can assemble to mate in a small pond. To the human ear their chorus may seem like a jumble of sounds, but the females pick out the call of their own species and follow it.

Smell and color also probably help bring male and female salamanders together. Many salamanders are brightly colored, so those of the same species can recognize one another by color markings.

DID YOU KNOW

**Jeepers, Peepers**

A chorus of spring peepers is organized into trios. All it takes to start the singing is for one peeper to call. A few moments later, one, and then another peeper joins in. In time, other trios pick up the song. Very quickly, all the peepers in the area are in full voice. If they are disturbed, the peeper choir stops. When the disturbance goes away, a peeper will begin to call again. Another will join, then a third. One, two, three, and every peeper is once more making frog music.

DID YOU KNOW

**Toad-al Chaos**

Many species of frogs and toads mate in large groups. Mating wood frogs can dot the entire surface of a small pond. Males dart about after females, rippling the water and splashing. Often, several males may try to climb on the back of a single female. She may kick and thrash about to keep from being pushed under the water's surface. All the while, males push and shove one another. It may be reproduction, but it looks like chaos.

The male American toad puffs out its vocal sac in order to call a mating partner. The male will continue to call until a female toad answers by approaching and showing that she is ready to mate.

## *Mating*

Having answered the call of the male frog, or having sniffed out the male salamander or identified it from its bright colors, the female amphibian is now ready to mate with the male of its species. During mating, the male sex cell—the sperm—unites with the female sex cell, the egg. A new animal arises from the union.

The eggs of frogs and toads are fertilized outside the female's body. The male climbs onto the female's back and holds her behind her front legs. In some species, such as the American toad, the male's thumbs grow larger at mating time, helping him to get a better grip. The female releases eggs from an opening at her rear that leads to the cloaca. The male then fertilizes the eggs by releasing sperm on them.

Most salamanders mate differently than frogs and toads. They have no mating calls, but many will perform a unique dance resembling a kind of underwater ballet. Spotted salamanders twist and turn around one another. The male red-spotted newt rubs against the female, then holds her behind the head with his rear legs.

When the dance is over, the male goes to the bottom of the water and deposits tiny cone-shaped capsules called spermatophores. Sperm from the male caps each spermatophore. The female then follows and puts her cloaca over each of the sperm caps. The sperm are attracted chemically to the walls of the cloaca. When the female releases eggs, they are fertilized. This is known as internal fertilization, as opposed to external fertilization, the method that is used by frogs and toads.

Not much is known about the mating habits of caecilians. As with salamanders, fertilization takes place internally in most species. The male deposits sperm in the female cloaca with his cloaca. Most caecilians lay eggs, but some produce live young.

The number of eggs a female amphibian produces depends on the species. The American toad lays from 5,000 to 10,000 eggs. The bullfrog lays up to 20,000. The gray tree frog lays only 30 to 40.

*Top*: The eggs of frogs and toads are fertilized outside of the female's body. To achieve fertilization, the male climbs on top of the female's back and positions himself by holding her around the abdomen. *Bottom*: Most salamanders perform a special dance before fertilization. Underwater, males deposit capsules covered with sperm, called spermatophores. The females collect the spermatophores in their cloacas, where eggs are fertilized as they are released. The white objects seen here are spermatophores.

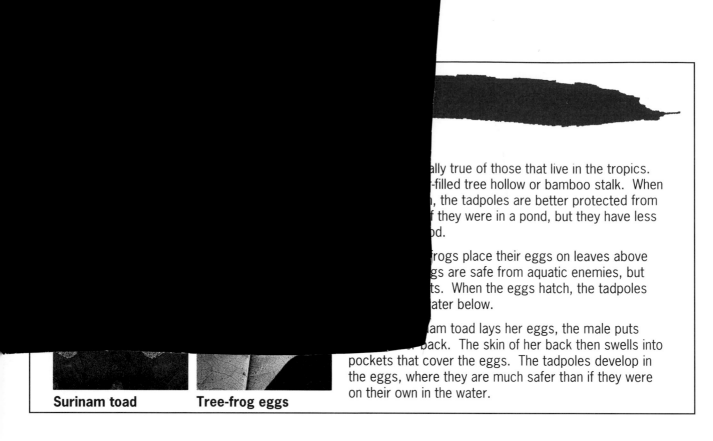

ally true of those that live in the tropics.
-filled tree hollow or bamboo stalk. When
, the tadpoles are better protected from
f they were in a pond, but they have less
d.

rogs place their eggs on leaves above
gs are safe from aquatic enemies, but
ts. When the eggs hatch, the tadpoles
ater below.

am toad lays her eggs, the male puts
back. The skin of her back then swells into
pockets that cover the eggs. The tadpoles develop in
the eggs, where they are much safer than if they were
on their own in the water.

**Surinam toad**     **Tree-frog eggs**

Some amphibians, such as the spring peeper and the cricket frog, lay eggs that stick to plants and leaves on the bottom of the water. Many others—the wood frog, for example—lay eggs in large clumps of jelly, attached to plants. The American toad's eggs are in a row within a string of jelly. Bullfrog eggs are contained within a film of jelly that floats on the water's surface.

## From Egg to Adult

A fertilized egg consists of a single cell at first. Soon, however, it divides into two cells, then four cells, and so forth, until there are millions of cells. The amphibian embryo, or developing organism, hatches into a tadpole (larva), usually within a few days to a month after fertilization. Once it hatches, a tadpole begins a process that will eventually turn it into an adult frog. This process is called metamorphosis, which means "change of shape." But more than just the tadpole's shape changes. Many of its organs also change, and the change is drastic.

DID YOU KNOW

**Hatch Me If You Can**

Frogs vary a great deal in the number of eggs they produce. Some species, such as the masked puddle frog, deposit eggs continuously throughout the year. Frogs that live in dry, harsh conditions may produce eggs only once a year. Hatch rates also vary from species to species. Some species hatch only one or two tadpoles at one time, while others can hatch up to 80,000 in one year!

# The Life Cycle of a Frog

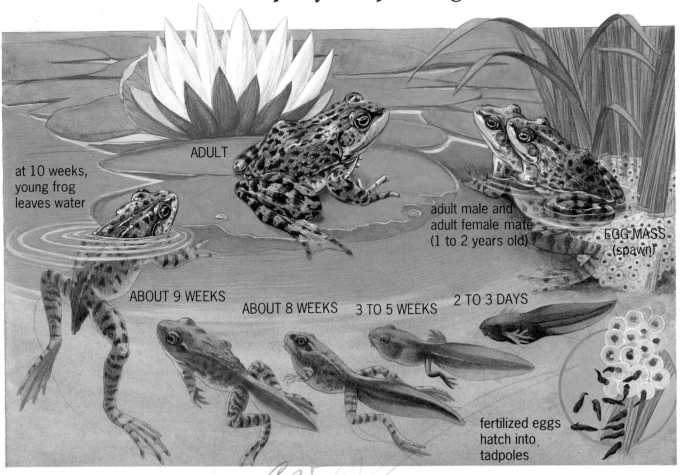

ADULT

at 10 weeks, young frog leaves water

adult male and adult female mate (1 to 2 years old)

EGG MASS (spawn)

ABOUT 9 WEEKS

ABOUT 8 WEEKS

3 TO 5 WEEKS

2 TO 3 DAYS

fertilized eggs hatch into tadpoles

A newly hatched frog tadpole resembles a tiny worm. After hatching, it rests on the bottom of the water, where its head enlarges. As weeks pass, more changes occur. Tiny hind legs sprout and begin to grow. Then the front legs start to grow, and the tadpole's lifestyle starts to change. As the left leg develops, it blocks the pore that empties water from the gills. The flow of water over the gills stops, and the gills stop functioning. Meanwhile, the tadpole has grown lungs to hold air it gulps at the water's surface.

In time, the tadpole's hind legs lengthen, its tail shrinks, and its intestines become shorter. When the young frog is ready to leave the water, its body is shaped like that of an adult, but it is smaller. The froglet, a sub-adult, will become a full adult when it is ready to mate. Amphibians usually reach mating age in a year or two, although some take longer.

DID YOU KNOW

**Stumped**

Many amphibian larvae have the astonishing ability to regrow limbs that have been injured or even cut off. Some adults, like the red-spotted newt, also have this ability. After a newt loses a leg, new skin forms over the stump. Scar tissue appears under the skin, which later disappears. In its place are cells similar to those that divide and form the newt embryo. These cells divide and form tissue. Scientists still do not fully understand the process, but eventually a new limb forms.

Reproduction and Growth

# 5

# Fitting into the Web of Life

 Every living thing must be able to survive in its own unique environment. How an organism looks, how its body works, and how it behaves are all connected to the kind of environment in which it must live. An organism's environment is made up of a number of different elements, including the land, food sources, and other living things. In a healthy environment, these elements create a natural balance for all things that live together in the same place.

## Eating...and Being Eaten

Amphibians eat just about any animal they can kill. They are also the food of almost any animal that can kill them. The list of amphibian enemies goes on and on. Tadpoles fall victim to large water insects, such as dragonfly larvae. A host of birds, such as herons and egrets, catch frogs, as do rat snakes. Hognose snakes

*Opposite:*
A green frog lies submerged in a sea of duckweed. Every living thing must adapt to its environment in a number of ways in order to survive.

**45**

feed on toads. Raccoons and otters feast on frogs and salamanders, as do largemouth bass, alligators, and snapping turtles.

## *Adapting to Changing Seasons*

To survive during the winter, when temperatures are cold and food is scarce, amphibians that live in temperate climates go into a "winter sleep" called hibernation. During hibernation, the animal's bodily activities—breathing, digestion, excretion, and circulation—slow down. Some frogs hide under logs or in crevices, while others burrow in mud at the bottoms of ponds. Toads burrow in the ground, sometimes as far down as 12 inches (30 centimeters). Salamanders winter in rotting tree stumps, under rocks in streams, or in damp burrows.

Amphibians that live in hot places must also adapt to temperature changes. When it becomes extremely hot and dry, they go into a "summer sleep," a period known as estivation. Estivation is similar to hibernation. Bodily functions slow down greatly as amphibians bury themselves in mud.

## *Defense in the Natural World*

Amphibians—except for the largest species—are not well equipped to fight off enemies. They have no claws or large teeth, no antlers, or horns; and most of them are relatively small. But they do have a number of other ways to defend themselves.

**Movement** Staying still is an amphibian's first line of defense. Whenever an amphibian senses the approach of something dangerous, it freezes in place. It even stops movements connected with breathing. Amphibians move very carefully even if they do not sense the danger. A toad will creep along for a short distance, then stop and remain still for a few moments before moving on.

Fitting into the Web of Life

When startled, amphibians often react by trying to sneak under cover. If they cannot, they quickly try to put distance between themselves and the enemy. Frogs, with their leaping ability, are best at this sort of defense. A bullfrog that is 8 inches (20 centimeters) long can leap 6 feet (2 meters). A leopard frog that is five inches (13 centimeters) long can jump almost as far.

Salamanders are not built for quick movement. Some, however, can jump by using their tail as a lever, striking it against the ground as they spring. In this way, a salamander can jump about the length of its body. That may not seem very far, but the quick movement can distract or confuse an enemy, allowing the salamander a chance to escape.

**Chemical warfare** Some amphibians, especially toads, use chemical warfare to defend themselves. Glands in their skin produce substances that can

A horned frog sits motionless on the forest floor. Most amphibians avoid danger by freezing all their body functions and blending with the surroundings as much as possible.

irritate or even poison creatures that attack them. Two very large glands can be seen on the head of the American toad, to the rear of its eyes. The secretions of the American toad irritate mucous membranes, such as those in the mouth. Because of this, many animals that pick up an American toad in their jaws drop it instantly. The hognose snake and striped skunk, however, do not seem to be bothered by the toad's secretions. They regularly kill and eat toads. You will not be harmed by touching a toad, but you should wash your hands thoroughly before touching your eyes or mouth.

The secretions of the giant toad found in the American tropics are much more powerful than those of the American toad. Dogs—even people—that have tried to eat this toad have died.

Many frogs and toads of the tropics secrete powerful poisons to discourage possible predators. The arrow-poison frog's skin is covered with a poison that is about 20 times stronger than any other dart frog's and can cause serious harm—even death—to humans.

## Poison Darts, That Smarts!

Many of the most brightly colored creatures in nature are also some of the most dangerous. The most brilliantly colored frogs, for example, are commonly the most poisonous. For centuries, hunters in the rain forests of Central and South America have used the poison from tropical frogs as an aid to hunting. To collect the poison, hunters must first roast an arrow-poison frog over a fire. As the frog roasts, the skin drips tiny drops of poison, which is collected in a container. Later, the tips of arrows are dipped into the poison before they are used for hunting. A poison-dipped arrow can instantly paralyze a number of small and medium-sized animals.

**Tropical arrow-poison frog**

Even more powerful are the skin secretions of a group of small, brightly colored South American frogs. They are called arrow-poison, or dart, frogs, and for a very good reason. Native Americans living in the rain forest make a deadly poison from the skin of these frogs. They place the poison on the points of their arrows and blow gun darts used in hunting. A monkey hit by one of these weapons is immediately paralyzed.

In 1978, scientists reported a new species of arrow-poison frog far more poisonous than any known before. The scientists warned that this frog should be handled with great care. If only a fraction of the poison enters a person's bloodstream—through a cut, for example—the person will die.

**Color changes** Natural camouflage, or blending in with the surroundings, helps an animal to hide from its enemies.

A gray tree frog, for example, that is the color of tree bark, blends in perfectly when it freezes on a tree trunk. The gray tree frog's skin color can also adjust to a lighter background. Against bark, dark-colored cells in the tree frog's skin expand. Against a light background, however, they contract, revealing cells with lighter colors.

Some amphibians, instead of hiding themselves with their colors, can confuse or startle their enemies

The Malaysian leaf frog is a master of camouflage. When it freezes in fear on a leaf or on the forest floor, it can barely be detected by an enemy.

**DID YOU KNOW**

**Attack of the Killer Frogs**

Some frogs have so much poison in their bodies that they can kill an amazing number of creatures. *Phyllobates terribilis*, one of the largest poisonous frogs, produces enough poison to kill about 20,000 laboratory mice with its poison.

by suddenly showing bright colors. Such colors are called warning coloration.

Arrow-poison frogs are among the most colorful animals alive. Their colors are readily visible. Sometimes, however, a poisonous amphibian hides its colors until disturbed. The fire-bellied toad of Europe and Asia is mostly gray in color. But when alarmed, the animal bends back its body, revealing bright orange spots beneath. The North American pickerel frog also has secretions that are poisonous to some other creatures. The inside surface of its legs are bright yellow. The yellow cannot be seen when the frog is at rest. When it jumps, however, the yellow flashes, then vanishes as the frog lands. This sudden show of bright color can be very startling and confusing to an enemy.

**Fooling the enemy** Amphibians have a number of other interesting ways to avoid being eaten. Frogs and toads can puff themselves up by filling their lungs with air. This change in appearance not only confuses the enemy, but it can also make the animal too big to be swallowed.

Some amphibians play dead. The leopard frog holds its breath when captured, and the enemy, thinking that its prey is dead, drops the frog.

A frog can also fool an enemy by emptying its bladder, the sac in which urine is stored, as it jumps away from the predator. The urine is distasteful to an enemy and, in addition, covers up the frog's scent. Moreover, the loud scream uttered by a frog as it jumps away or when it is picked up roughly is so startling that animals that grab frogs in their jaws will often drop them.

Some frogs and toads can puff themselves up in order to discourage predators. The tomato frog can fill itself with air to make itself harder to swallow or to make an enemy think its prey is larger than it really is.

Many salamanders have a kind of detachable tail that allows them to escape their enemies. If a salamander has its tail grabbed, the tail will break off, allowing the animal to escape. After a few weeks, a new tail will often grow back.

Many salamanders sacrifice their tail in order to escape enemies. If a predator grabs one of these salamanders by the tail, it breaks off, neatly and cleanly. The tail keeps wiggling after it breaks away. While the predator is occupied by the squirming tail, the salamander escapes. These salamanders can usually grow new tails.

## The Human Connection to Amphibians

Like most other living things, amphibians interact with people. Because most amphibians are small and often hidden, however, people are less aware of them than they are of other organisms, like insects or mammals. Most people do not recognize how important amphibians are, and they also don't realize the extent to which human activities affect amphibians.

**Pest control** Amphibians are a group of natural pest controllers. By eating insects, they destroy hordes of insect pests. What's more, amphibians work the "night shift," when most insect-eating birds are asleep.

## Let's Pander to the Salamander

Not all human activities hurt amphibians. Amphibians often breed in ponds dug by farmers to water cattle. Some amphibians even breed in cattle troughs. To protect amphibians, some people put up "Salamander Crossing" signs on roads near breeding ponds. The signs warn drivers to watch out for salamanders, which sometimes cross such roads in large numbers on wet spring nights.

It was once estimated that a single toad is worth $50 a year to a farmer because of the crops it saves from insects.

**Research** Frogs have played an important role in science. In the eighteenth century, Italian anatomy professor Luigi Galvani used a frog's leg to show that chemical action could produce an electrical current. When he touched the leg with two different metals, the electrical charge that went through the nerves and muscles made the leg contract. Eventually, Galvani's discovery led to the invention of the electric battery.

Because frogs are basic vertebrates, they have been widely used in biological research and education. Countless students have learned about the structure and workings of the vertebrate body by dissecting frogs. Laboratory studies on amphibian tadpoles have provided considerable information on the growth and development of vertebrates.

Scientists are now studying a common disease of frogs and toads called "redleg." The immune system of frogs and toads normally protects them against the disease. But when their immune system breaks down, they can die from this disease. Similarly, when a person is infected with AIDS, the failure of the immune system turns normally mild infections into life-threatening ones. No one knows what causes the immune systems of frogs and toads to fail, but scientists are looking for the reason.

**Wart's Up?**

For a long time, many people believed that touching toads would give a person warts. Today, scientists know that frogs and toads do not cause warts any more than touching a cat! (But you should always wash your hands after handling a frog or a toad because the oils on their skin can sometimes irritate the eyes or mouth.)

**Interesting subjects** Frogs have also been the subjects of great works of writing. In ancient Greece, frogs were the main "characters" in some of Aesop's fables, and one Greek wrote a play called *The Frogs.* Famed American author Mark Twain wrote a humorous story called *The Celebrated Jumping Frog of Calaveras County.* It is why people from all over bring frogs to Calaveras, in California, for an annual frog-jumping contest.

**As pets and food** Amphibians, while not as common as cats and dogs in the home, can make very interesting pets. Tadpoles kept in an aquarium provide the curious with a vivid demonstration of metamorphosis. Native peoples in many parts of the world also rely on various amphibians for food. In many countries, frog legs are considered a delicacy. Conservationists warn, however, that capturing frogs for food must be strictly controlled in order to protect various species from being overhunted and threatened with possible extinction.

## Amphibians in Danger

For a long time, the number of amphibians has been dropping. At present, 45 species are in danger of becoming extinct. Many of the same human activities that threaten other animals also put amphibians in danger of extinction. Removing them from the wild for commercial and scientific purposes—even for pets—has hurt some species. Pollution, such as acid rain, has poisoned many amphibian breeding waters. Development and agriculture have also destroyed many habitats. Filling in wetlands or damming them up has been very damaging to amphibians. The real-estate or commercial development of areas that once contained water-filled areas for breeding has also hurt amphibian populations.

When amphibians decrease, other animals suffer. Less food is available for the many creatures that eat amphibians. The loss of amphibians could destroy entire food chains—and harm people. Vast numbers of frogs have been killed for food in Bangladesh, a country in Asia. As a result, Bangladesh is now alive with mosquitoes, which spread the disease malaria.

In recent years, amphibians seem to be disappearing over wide areas at an ever-faster rate. North America's western toad numbers have dropped 80 percent since the late 1970s. Thousands of golden toads once bred in a Costa Rican rain forest, but in 1988 scientists saw only one golden toad there, and

The Chinese giant salamander has become an endangered species because a number of human activities have destroyed its natural habitat. The effects of pollution and land development threaten thousands of living things by disrupting food chains, water supplies, and breeding grounds.

A delicate glass frog clings to a branch in the Costa Rican rain forest. Because rain forests are some of the world's richest habitats, their destruction threatens thousands of species.

DID YOU KNOW

**Too Rude to Brood**

The gastric brooding frog is one of the endangered amphibians and may even be extinct. This is unfortunate, since scientists are very curious about one special ability of the female gastric brooder. Tadpoles develop in her stomach, but when they are ready to hatch, they jump right out of her mouth!

none has been spotted since. In 1980, the population of an Australian frog species went underground for the winter. It never appeared again. And the Cascades frog, from California, also seems to have disappeared.

What is killing the amphibians? Scientists are eager to know. It could be a temporary decline, which sometimes occurs in certain animal populations, but usually not on a global basis.

Acid rain and pesticides may be at least partly to blame. Some scientists suspect that increased ultra-violet light, which is let in by the destruction of the Earth's ozone layer, may be at fault.

Whatever is causing amphibians to disappear, it is not good news for us. We share the world with amphibians, so if something in the environment is killing them, eventually it might do the same to us. We must all remember that, when the environment is unhealthy, all living things will eventually have to pay the price.

Fitting into the Web of Life

# Classification Chart of Amphibians

**Kingdom: Animal**
**Phylum: Chordata**
**Class: Amphibia**

Scientists have identified more than 4,000 species of amphibians. These species are classified into three orders.

| Order | Common Members | Distinctive Features |
|-------|----------------|----------------------|
| Anura "without a tail" | frogs, toads | tailless; short body; long hind legs adapted for hopping; eggs fertilized outside body; on all continents except Antarctica, but most abundant in the tropics |
| Urodela "creatures with visible tails" | salamanders, newts | tail; most with long body; voiceless; eggs fertilized inside body; most abundant in Northern Hemisphere |
| Apoda "without feet" | caecilians | legless; long body with surface grooved into a series of ring-like segments and some with scales; blind or nearly so; eggs fertilized inside body in most species; found in tropics only |

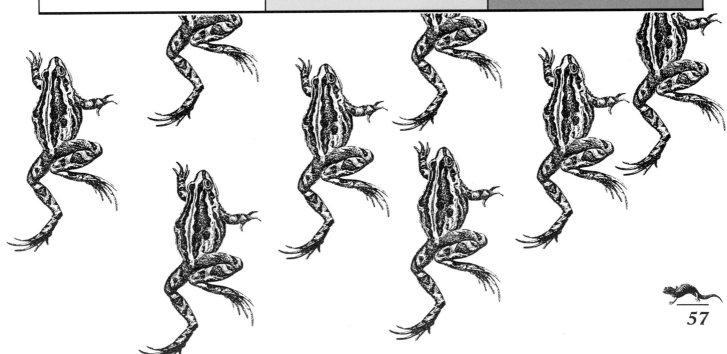

# THE ANIMAL KINGDOM

| Porifera SPONGES | Cnidaria COELENTERATES | Platyhelminthes FLATWORMS | Nematoda ROUNDWORMS | Mollusca MOLLUSKS | Annelida TRUE WORMS |

**Cnidaria:**
- Hydrozoa HYDRAS, HYDROIDS
- Scyphozoa JELLYFISH
- Anthozoa SEA ANEMONES, CORALS

**Platyhelminthes:**
- Turbellaria FREE-LIVING FLATWORMS
- Monogenea PARASITIC FLUKES
- Trematoda PARASITIC FLUKES
- Cestoda TAPEWORMS

**Mollusca:**
- Polyplacophora CHITONS
- Gastropoda SNAILS, SLUGS
- Bivalvia CLAMS, SCALLOPS, MUSSELS
- Cephalopoda OCTOPUSES, SQUID

**Annelida:**
- Polychaeta MARINE WORMS
- Oligochaeta EARTHWORMS, FRESHWATER WORMS
- Hirudinea LEECHES

## Biological Classification

The branch of biology that deals with classification is called taxonomy, or systematics. Biological classification is the arrangement of living organisms into categories. Biologists have created a universal system of classification that they can share with one another, no matter where they study or what language they speak. The categories in a classification chart are based on the natural similarities of the organisms. The similarities considered are the structure of the organism, the development (reproduction and growth), biochemical and physiological functions (metabolism and senses), and evolutionary history. Biologists classify living things to show relationships between different groups of organisms, both ancient and modern. Classification charts are also useful in tracing the evolutionary pathways along which present-day organisms have evolved.

Over the years, the classification process has been altered as new information has become accepted. A long time ago, biologists used a two-kingdom system of classification; every living thing was considered a member of either the plant kingdom or the animal kingdom. Today, many biologists use a five-kingdom system that includes plants, animals, monera (microbes), protista (protozoa and certain molds), and fungi (non-green plants). In every kingdom, however, the hierarchy of classification remains the same. In this chart, groupings go from the most general categories (at the top) down to groups that are more and more specific. The most general grouping is PHYLUM. The most specific is ORDER. To use the chart, you may want to find the familiar name of an organism in a CLASS or ORDER box and then trace its classification upward until you reach its PHYLUM.

**Arthropoda classes:**
- Insecta INSECTS
- Chilopoda CENTIPEDES
- Diplopoda MILLIPEDES
- Symphyla, Pauropoda SYMPHYLANS, PAUROPODS

**Insecta orders:**

Collembola, SPRINGTAILS
Thysanura, SILVERFISH, BRISTLETAILS
Ephemeroptera, MAYFLIES
Odonata, DRAGONFLIES, DAMSELFLIES
Isoptera, TERMITES
Orthoptera, LOCUSTS, CRICKETS, GRASSHOPPERS
Dictyoptera, COCKROACHES, MANTIDS
Dermaptera, EARWIGS
Phasmida, STICK INSECTS, LEAF INSECTS
Psocoptera, BOOK LICE, BARK LICE
Diplura, SIMPLE INSECTS
Protura, TELSONTAILS
Plecoptera, STONEFLIES
Grylloblattodea, TINY MOUNTAIN INSECTS
Strepsiptera, TWISTED-WINGED STYLOPIDS
Trichoptera, CADDIS FLIES
Embioptera, WEBSPINNERS
Thysanoptera, THRIPS
Mecoptera, SCORPION FLIES
Zoraptera, RARE TROPICAL INSECTS
Hemiptera, TRUE BUGS
Anoplura, SUCKING LICE
Mallophaga, BITING LICE, BIRD LICE
Homoptera, WHITE FLIES, APHIDS, SCALE INSECTS, CICADAS
Coleoptera, BEETLES, WEEVILS
Neuroptera, ALDERFLIES, LACEWINGS, ANT LIONS, SNAKE FLIES, DOBSONFLIES
Hymenoptera, ANTS, BEES, WASPS
Siphonaptera, FLEAS
Diptera, TRUE FLIES, MOSQUITOES, GNATS
Lepidoptera, BUTTERFLIES, MOTHS

**Mammalia orders:**

Insectivora, INSECTIVORES (e.g., shrews, moles, hedgehogs)
Chiroptera, BATS
Dermoptera, FLYING LEMURS
Edentata, ANTEATERS, SLOTHS, ARMADILLOS
Pholidota, PANGOLINS
Primates, PROSIMIANS (e.g., lemurs, tarsiers, monkeys, apes, humans)
Rodentia, RODENTS (e.g., squirrels, rats, beavers, mice, porcupines)
Lagomorpha, RABBITS, HARES, PIKAS
Cetacea, WHALES, DOLPHINS, PORPOISES
Carnivora, CARNIVORES (e.g., cats, dogs, weasels, bears, hyenas)
Pinnipedia, SEALS, SEA LIONS, WALRUSES
Tubulidentata, AARDVARKS
Hyracoidea, HYRAXES
Proboscidea, ELEPHANTS
Sirenia, SEA COWS (e.g., manatees, dugongs)
Perissodactyla, ODD-TOED HOOFED MAMMALS (e.g., horses, rhinoceroses, tapirs)
Artiodactyla, EVEN-TOED HOOFED MAMMALS (e.g., hogs, cattle, camels, hippopotamuses)

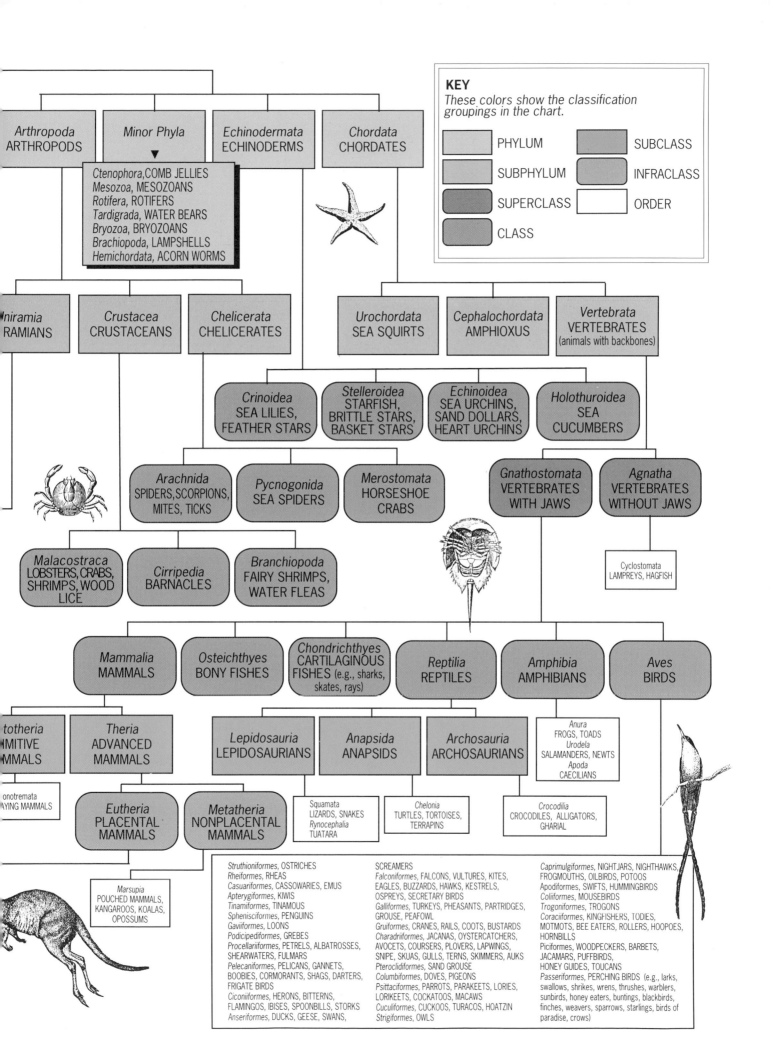

**KEY**

These colors show the classification groupings in the chart.

- PHYLUM
- SUBPHYLUM
- SUPERCLASS
- CLASS
- SUBCLASS
- INFRACLASS
- ORDER

*Arthropoda* ARTHROPODS

*Minor Phyla* ▼

*Ctenophora,* COMB JELLIES
*Mesozoa,* MESOZOANS
*Rotifera,* ROTIFERS
*Tardigrada,* WATER BEARS
*Bryozoa,* BRYOZOANS
*Brachiopoda,* LAMPSHELLS
*Hemichordata,* ACORN WORMS

*Echinodermata* ECHINODERMS

*Chordata* CHORDATES

*niramia* RAMIANS

*Crustacea* CRUSTACEANS

*Chelicerata* CHELICERATES

*Urochordata* SEA SQUIRTS

*Cephalochordata* AMPHIOXUS

*Vertebrata* VERTEBRATES (animals with backbones)

*Crinoidea* SEA LILIES, FEATHER STARS

*Stelleroidea* STARFISH, BRITTLE STARS, BASKET STARS

*Echinoidea* SEA URCHINS, SAND DOLLARS, HEART URCHINS

*Holothuroidea* SEA CUCUMBERS

*Arachnida* SPIDERS, SCORPIONS, MITES, TICKS

*Pycnogonida* SEA SPIDERS

*Merostomata* HORSESHOE CRABS

*Gnathostomata* VERTEBRATES WITH JAWS

*Agnatha* VERTEBRATES WITHOUT JAWS

*Cyclostomata* LAMPREYS, HAGFISH

*Malacostraca* LOBSTERS, CRABS, SHRIMPS, WOOD LICE

*Cirripedia* BARNACLES

*Branchiopoda* FAIRY SHRIMPS, WATER FLEAS

*Mammalia* MAMMALS

*Osteichthyes* BONY FISHES

*Chondrichthyes* CARTILAGINOUS FISHES (e.g., sharks, skates, rays)

*Reptilia* REPTILES

*Amphibia* AMPHIBIANS

*Aves* BIRDS

*totheria* MITIVE MMALS

*Theria* ADVANCED MAMMALS

*Lepidosauria* LEPIDOSAURIANS

*Anapsida* ANAPSIDS

*Archosauria* ARCHOSAURIANS

*Anura* FROGS, TOADS
*Urodela* SALAMANDERS, NEWTS
*Apoda* CAECILIANS

*onotremata* AYING MAMMALS

*Eutheria* PLACENTAL MAMMALS

*Metatheria* NONPLACENTAL MAMMALS

*Squamata* LIZARDS, SNAKES
*Rynocephalia* TUATARA

*Chelonia* TURTLES, TORTOISES, TERRAPINS

*Crocodilia* CROCODILES, ALLIGATORS, GHARIAL

*Marsupia* POUCHED MAMMALS, KANGAROOS, KOALAS, OPOSSUMS

*Struthioniformes,* OSTRICHES
*Rheiformes,* RHEAS
*Casuariiformes,* CASSOWARIES, EMUS
*Apterygiformes,* KIWIS
*Tinamiformes,* TINAMOUS
*Sphenisciformes,* PENGUINS
*Gaviiformes,* LOONS
*Podicipediformes,* GREBES
*Procellariiformes,* PETRELS, ALBATROSSES, SHEARWATERS, FULMARS
*Pelecaniformes,* PELICANS, GANNETS, BOOBIES, CORMORANTS, SHAGS, DARTERS, FRIGATE BIRDS
*Ciconiiformes,* HERONS, BITTERNS, FLAMINGOS, IBISES, SPOONBILLS, STORKS
*Anseriformes,* DUCKS, GEESE, SWANS,

SCREAMERS
*Falconiformes,* FALCONS, VULTURES, KITES, EAGLES, BUZZARDS, HAWKS, KESTRELS, OSPREYS, SECRETARY BIRDS
*Galliformes,* TURKEYS, PHEASANTS, PARTRIDGES, GROUSE, PEAFOWL
*Gruiformes,* CRANES, RAILS, COOTS, BUSTARDS
*Charadriiformes,* JACANAS, OYSTERCATCHERS, AVOCETS, COURSERS, PLOVERS, LAPWINGS, SNIPE, SKUAS, GULLS, TERNS, SKIMMERS, AUKS
*Pteroclidiformes,* SAND GROUSE
*Columbiformes,* DOVES, PIGEONS
*Psittaciformes,* PARROTS, PARAKEETS, LORIES, LORIKEETS, COCKATOOS, MACAWS
*Cuculiformes,* CUCKOOS, TURACOS, HOATZIN
*Strigiformes,* OWLS

*Caprimulgiformes,* NIGHTJARS, NIGHTHAWKS, FROGMOUTHS, OILBIRDS, POTOOS
*Apodiformes,* SWIFTS, HUMMINGBIRDS
*Coliiformes,* MOUSEBIRDS
*Trogoniformes,* TROGONS
*Coraciiformes,* KINGFISHERS, TODIES, MOTMOTS, BEE EATERS, ROLLERS, HOOPOES, HORNBILLS
*Piciformes,* WOODPECKERS, BARBETS, JACAMARS, PUFFBIRDS, HONEY GUIDES, TOUCANS
*Passeriformes,* PERCHING BIRDS (e.g., larks, swallows, shrikes, wrens, thrushes, warblers, sunbirds, honey eaters, buntings, blackbirds, finches, weavers, sparrows, starlings, birds of paradise, crows)

# Glossary

**atria** The two top chambers of the heart, through which blood flows to the ventricle.

**camouflage** The colors, shapes, or structures that enable an organism to blend with its surroundings.

**cloaca** The structure in an amphibian into which the digestive, urinary, and reproductive systems open.

**cones** Light-sensitive cells in the eye that are most sensitive in bright light and register color.

**digestion** The mechanical and chemical breakdown of food into substances the body can use for growth and energy.

**dormancy** A period of rest during either very hot or cold weather, when bodily functions slow down.

**embryo** The young organism developing from a fertilized egg.

**esophagus** The structure through which food passes from the mouth to the stomach.

**estivation** A period of rest during very hot weather when the body processes slow down.

**evolve** To develop over a long period of time.

**excretion** The removal from the body of wastes that are created during metabolism.

**exhale** To breathe out.

**extinct** No longer in existence.

**fertilize** The union of sperm and egg, which leads to the development of a new organism.

**gills** The organs that a tadpole uses to breathe.

**habitat** The particular part of the environment in which an organism lives.

**hibernation** A period of rest during very cold weather when the body processes slow down.

**hormones** Chemicals that regulate body processes.

**immune system** A collection of cells and proteins that protects the body against disease.

**larva** A newly hatched amphibian; a tadpole.

**larynx** The organ that produces voice.

**lateral line** An organ along each side of some amphibians' bodies that senses very low vibrations and serves as an extended sense of touch.

**lens** A clear structure at the center of the eye through which light passes to the retina.

**metabolism** The chemical processes in cells that are essential to life.

**metamorphosis** The physical development and changes that transform an egg to a tadpole and then into an adult amphibian.

**molecule** The smallest particle of a substance that retains all the properties of the substance.

**nictitating membrane** A clear membrane that can be brought across the amphibian eye to protect it and keep vision clear in water.

**papillae** Tiny projections that sense touch.

**predator** An animal that kills other animals.

**prey** An animal that is eaten by another animal.

**reproduction** The process by which organisms create other members of their species.

**respiration** The exchange of gases between an organism and its environment; the use of oxygen by the tissues and cells of the body.

**retina** A light-sensitive coating on the back of the eye like the film of a camera.

**rods** Light-sensitive cells in the back of the eye that are most sensitive in dim light and register only black and white.

**sensory nerves** Nerves that carry messages from the sense organs to the brain.

**species** A group of organisms that share more traits with one another than with other organisms and that can reproduce with one another.

**sperm** The male reproductive cell that fertilizes a female egg.

**stimuli** Messages received by an animal's senses from its surroundings.

**tadpole** The organism that hatches from a frog or toad egg.

**ventricle** The lower chamber of the amphibian's heart that sends blood to the lungs and body.

**vertebrate** An animal with a backbone.

# For Further Reading

Bailey, Donna. *What We Can Do About Protecting Nature*. New York: Franklin Watts, 1992.

Clarke, Barry. *Amphibian*. New York: Alfred A. Knopf, 1993.

Dallinger, Jane, and Johnson, Sylvia. *Frogs and Toads*. Minneapolis, MN: Lerner, 1982.

Ganeri, Anita. *Rivers, Ponds & Lakes*. New York: Macmillan Children's Group, 1992.

George, Jean C. *The Moon of the Salamanders*. New York: HarperCollins Children's Books, 1992.

Headstrom, Richard. *Adventures with Freshwater Animals*. New York: Dover, 1983.

Jennings, Terry. *Pond Life*. Chicago, IL: Childrens Press, 1989.

Johnson, Sylvia. *Tree Frogs*. Minneapolis, MN: Lerner, 1986.

Losito, Linda. *Reptiles & Amphibians*. New York: Facts On File, 1989.

Mason, Helen. *Life in a Pond*. Niagra Falls, NY: Durkin Hayes, 1992.

Minelli, Giuseppe. *Amphibians*. New York: Facts On File, 1987.

Oda, Hidetomo. *The Tadpole*. Madison, NJ: Raintree Steck-Vaughn, 1986.

Oda, Hidetomo. *The Tree Frog*. Madison, NJ: Raintree Steck-Vaughn, 1986.

Sabin, Francene. *Ecosystems and Food Chains*. Mahwah, NJ: Troll Associates, 1985.

Seidenberg, Steven. *Ecology and Conservation*. Milwaukee, WI: Gareth Stevens, 1990.

Snow, John. *Secrets of Ponds & Lakes*. Portland, ME: Gannett Books, 1982.

Steele, Philip. *Extinct Amphibians: And Those in Danger of Extinction*. New York: Franklin Watts, 1992.

Steele, Philip. *Reptiles & Amphibians*. New York: Julian Messner, 1991.

Tesar, Jenny. *Endangered Habitats*. New York: Facts On File, 1991.

Tesar, Jenny. *Shrinking Forests*. New York: Facts On File, 1991.

Wald, Mike. *What You Can Do for the Environment*. New York: Chelsea House, 1993.

Wiessinger, John R. *Fish, Frogs, & Snakes—Right Before Your Eyes*. Hillside, NJ: Enslow, 1989.

# *Index*

**Photo Credits**
Cover and title page: ©Joseph T. Collins/Photo Researchers, Inc.; p. 6: ©Gary Retherford/ Photo Researchers, Inc.; p. 8: ©Stephen Dalton/Photo Researchers, Inc. (left), ©John M. Burnley/Photo Researchers, Inc.; p. 9: ©Tom McHugh/Atlanta Zoo/Photo Researchers, Inc.; p. 10: ©Tom McHugh/Steinhart Aquarium/Photo Researchers, Inc.; p. 11: ©Dr. Paul A. Zahl/Photo Researchers, Inc. (both); p. 13: ©Suzanne L. Collins & Joseph T. Collins/ Photo Researchers, Inc. (left), ©Tom Michael P. Gadomski/Photo Researchers, Inc. (right); p. 14: ©Joseph T. Collins/Photo Researchers, Inc.; p. 17: ©Jeff Lepore/Photo Researchers, Inc.; p. 18: ©Stephen Dalton/Photo Researchers, Inc.; p. 20: ©Suzanne L. Collins & Joseph T. Collins/Photo Researchers, Inc.; p. 21: ©Herbert Schwind/OKAPIA/ Photo Researchers, Inc.; p. 23: ©William J. Jahoda/Photo Researchers, Inc.; p. 24: ©Nick Bergkessel/Photo Researchers, Inc.; p. 25: ©Jeff Lepore/Photo Researchers, Inc.; p. 27: ©Stephen Dalton/Photo Researchers, Inc.; p. 29: ©Tom McHugh/Photo Researchers, Inc.; p. 30: ©Ken Highfill/Photo Researchers, Inc.; p. 33: ©Scott Camazine/Photo Researchers, Inc.; p. 36: ©John Burnley/Photo Researchers, Inc.; p. 39: ©Alvin E. Staffan/Photo Researchers, Inc.; p. 40: ©Jeff Lepore/Photo Researchers, Inc.; p. 41: ©Jany Sauvanet/Photo Researchers, Inc. (top), ©J.L. Lepore/Photo Researchers, Inc. (bottom); p. 42: ©Tom McHugh/Steinhart Aquarium/Photo Researchers, Inc. (left), ©Gary Retherford/Photo Researchers, Inc. (right); p. 44: ©Rod Planck/Photo Researchers, Inc.; p. 47: ©Joseph T. Collins/Photo Researchers, Inc.; p. 48: ©Tom McHugh/Photo Researchers, Inc.; p. 49: ©Stephen J. Krasemann/Photo Researchers, Inc.; p. 50: ©E. R. Degginger/Photo Researchers, Inc.; p. 51: ©E. R. Degginger/Photo Researchers, Inc.; p. 52: ©Suzanne L. Collins & Joseph T. Collins/Photo Researchers, Inc.; p. 55: ©Tom McHugh/Photo Researchers, Inc.; p. 56: ©Tom McHugh/Steinhart Aquarium/Photo Researchers, Inc.

Technical illustrations: ©Blackbirch Press, Inc.